ALL THE
BARBARIC GLASS

ALL THE
BARBARIC GLASS

David Butler

Doire Press

First published in 2017

Doire Press
Aille, Inverin
Co. Galway
www.doirepress.com

Layout & cover design: Lisa Frank
Author photo: Tanya Farrelly
Cover painting: David Lee

Printed by Clódóirí CL
Casla, Co. na Gaillimhe

ISBN 978-1-907682-50-6

We gratefully acknowledge the assistance of The Arts Council / An Chomhairle Ealaíon.

CONTENTS

To the memory of my sister, Joan, whose support was unconditional.

Breaking

There are times you need
to step outside the colloquy;
to mute the looping newsfeed,
the tinnitus of the immediate.
Times, to step out from
the shadows criss-crossing
all the barbaric glass.

To know a cold wind hone
the moon to a scimitar;
a sea aglow with dusk;
to listen to the gossip of waves,
the hunger, the blood-course;
the seabird's ululation
across a desolate sunset.

Exodus

What bundle has morning washed up
on the shores of the internet,
a tiny Gulliver, though silent as stillbirth?
A Moses among the bullrushes?
Pharaoh has sent his towering guard
like the giant of Gallipoli, to raise him.
Surely, among all the suitcases, empty as grief,
that bob on the Aegean, one can be found
to cradle him, float him onwards…

Minatory

All night the tide, engorged, has charged,
foamed, bellowed, pawed at the shingle.
Morning has tamed it. The moon-faced girl
who plays amidst the detritus has
quite forgotten her terror now.

Idly she lines up shell and fragment
in the wrack. The sea is watching.

Could she read these runes, might she
thread through their maze the mounting
wave and undertow; the bestial swell
of obsession; the monstrous birth;
the black sail that drowns a father?

Misgiving

Your tiny hand sheds breadcrumbs
on the ale-stained mouth of the Dargle.
Brash as a bagpipe, a barnacle goose
waddles and honks and provokes
the mallards' guttural laughter.
An uncoiled swan throws a hissy-fit
where a sandpiper stole a march.
Why this ache of foreboding?

Sand-mites flit in the pubic wrack
where the hem of the tide has fallen;
where mussels like blue contusions
hold fast till the sea's return;
and a brazen cascade of gulls
unable to pass up the free-for-all
is coaxing a hundred creaky hinges
to cacophonous derision.

The Dogfish

The tide has thrown up a dogfish,
sandpaper-rough and dense as muscle;
a tough trial to the iridescent flies.

Outside the deaf-mute element
a parched wind filled with bird-shrieks
has begun a slow embalming.

Already it is eyeless. Small wonder
the child with bucket stands and stares
and starts to hear the song of sand;
the whisper in the hourglass.

Depredation

The drunken wind which last night
stomped through the playground,
drove the park into a frenzy
of soughing boughs, buffeted
the houses, sputtered
down the throats of chimneys,
chased cascades of startled
leaves against the windows, has,
this morning, taken a breather.
The ground is littered with all
the detritus of late autumn,
as if a carnival has decamped;
and the trees, stripped bare
as parents when grief tears through them,
are suddenly old.

And then the sun broke through

A sea of jade and muscatel; the sky, gun-metal.
Landward, the storm-portending birds, white-lit,
riding wild contours of wind, uplift
to tilt at the raucous crows. This
is how it is to live, the ticker tells,
looping the floor of the newsfeed.
Somewhere, an outrage, an airstrike;
somewhere, a politic withdrawal. This
is how it is to live: the wind blowing
the charcoal of crows' feathers;
the rent in the clouds; oblique tines beating
sudden ochre out of a sullen ocean.

These are the Dead Days

Into the nappy-warmth, the air
clammy with the taint of incontinence.
A grimace at the nurses' station,
at the ritual of the hand-sanitiser.
Then down long corridors, marigold, lilac,
to a room of kindergarten murals,
a dim realm held in the stupor of sleep
peopled by shades, mouths agape
to watch the slow descent to where he sits:
your father a child again.
Time is a scarab, that
backward rolls this dungy Earth.

Father

What unsigned city is it that you wake in,
featureless, or with such altered feature
the streets are not familiar, or if, with
shifting familiarity, like the dreamscapes
you wake from? What day is it, the moving ridge
hammered flat that separates past from future
so all is present tense, a watery time
in which the hours gradually dissolve?

How is it that memory, once so sharp,
has lost its stylus, and slides across the surface
leaving no impression but vague anxiety
that something isn't right? And who are we
who have come to ask you? Forgive us
this daily trespass through your threadless maze.

Watcher

i.m. my mother

I see you by the window,
ghosted in the pane over
a garden coarse with winter
fabric: khaki and hessian.
Beneath the gloomy leylandii,
the rowan, stripped of reds now.
There are starlings stabbing at
the water-heavy lawn,
rifling the blackened leaves
under the judas tree.

You ignore their racket.
Your eye is fixed here, where
seed hangs in fat gourds
to lure the liveried finches,
the coal-tits, a robin
round as a bauble;
and every visitor
welcome as a mummer
tumbling through your
own relentless winter.

Grandfather Clock

Years it stood, a Grand Inquisitor,
The embodiment of Victorian virtue:
Fortitude, say, or Perseverance;
The pendulum in its coffin
A scythe, severing Time
With each interrogative *Tick...?*
Then *Tock!,* its barbarous preterite,
Telling that the moment had fled;
Tolling that the moment had fled.

Alzheimer's

I've watched those eyes
enmeshed in time
abandon time;
and know your mind
has wandered down
to the nether shore,
where year on year
you await the oar.

Man of sand;
a relentless wind
is whittling you over
to that farther shore,
grain after grain,
after my mother.

Ráithín an Chloig, Bray

All day a louring sky has squatted
low on the slate-grey horizon.
Under its sombre light, the sea
is beaten metal, tarnished, unannealed,
sending slow scallops landward.
The brae is in winter livery:
bare furze, tree-fern and bracken.
I've climbed to this silence again.
The waves of hundreds of years
have broken and regathered
since Bray last heard a bell here
inside this open ruin, roofless,
mute as a cleft palate,
from which faith, a lost language,
has long since flown.

Correspondences

Brambles are nature's graffiti, staking
claims over ruined walls; stalking tranches
of no-man's-land; each pubic tangle
a challenge and retort. Their barbs
hold no terrors for the birds, though,
which flit in and out and burst
the silence with their belligerence,
each to its own. There are more
tongues here than in a metropolis:
gorse and cowslip and insect
all flash their intimate semaphore;
a corncrake croaks morse; while a skylark
hoisted high as a radio-mast,
is twittering its incessant machine-code.

Dream of Insects

I

cricket, cricket
light as thought,
light as air,
leg a hair-trigger
sprung by a stare;
now a-chirrup,
now afloat over a long green summer

II

electrically intermittent
the dry isles' insistent tinnitus:
cicadas sizzle from each parched bark;
the hysterical racket is sex-mad;
heat ratchets its stiff intensity:
listen listen listen listen

III

locust; old man;
husk of want; chaff;
winged hunger;
numerous as
the host of
the dead,
rising from the bones of the land
like Famine.

Cartographers

Uncertain only as to which monarch
would underwrite their madness
their loyalty was maritime:
the gnawing breeze, the prow's
surge and fall that scattered
hoar over the trackless ocean.
Their intimacy was with trade and line,
with the minute limit of the azimuth,
and the slow tilt of constellations.
What hunger impelled them
to cast fortune to the winds
and cross the uncharted horizon?

Upon those shores that vindicated their folly
they left their indifferent flags, like spores.

Ten Miniatures

[1] Of Love and Language

Herod the Great, they say,
had his beloved Mariamne
entombed in honey; as amber traps
the hapless fly in its perfect retina.

Words are benign, dealing in categories.
Only the lover and the artist
have such Medusa eyes.

[2] Seascape with Tempest

No more than a squall: slant
rain-walls embracing vacancy;
the sea needlessly flexing, its
seething unheeded in the ear
of the gale until a fleck,
two-masted and listing,
brings the scene to focus.

[3] Cat's Eye

City lights quiver like aspen leaves
in the slow liquorice river.
The wind has shivered a glass half-moon
into shimmering slivers,
into silver elver scribbling under where,
catlike, the Ha'penny Bridge
has over-arched its old arch-rival.

[4] Harbour Miniature

Evening settles like a fire in a brazier.
The sun, prodigal to the last, has touched
with a glazier's brush the porcelain waves.
Everything wet or metal has been fired
and winks red-eyed at the dark, in
which gulls, brazen, float as over a kiln
whose door has been thrown wide open.

[5] Hermit Crab

Mind is a hermit crab;
fingers without a hand
that scuttle through detritus;
scavenger; salvage-merchant
inhabiting such shards it finds
along the savage foreshore,
discards of older forms.

[6] All the Dead Voices

Evening. A tree. A rock. Though that's not right.
No stage is bare. Memory inhabits it.
Here, and here, the hoisted loy;
the six lost characters; the crouch-back pretender.
No stage is bare. It is Venice; or a tenement;
or a state of mind. *Fade to black.* Whispers
rustle in the wings, like feathers, like leaves.

[7] **Ghost Writer**

I would be bone, says the birch,
bark wrapped in tissue
thin as papered garlic.
I would worship the fossil moon
that haunts cerulean day.
I would be boon friend of the owl,
blanched and stealthy, as Death.

[8] In Memoriam

Their month is November, disdainful of generation.
The pollarded cross; the blood-poppy
paper-thin in the indifferent wind.
Old testament to a graven god,
who is it we must not forget?
The inestimable dead? Or the returned
who did not grow old as we grow old?

[9] Starlings over Piazza Cinquecento

Variations on a theme in Dante:
souls in cosmic callisthenics.
Harmonic motion; galaxies'
gravitational flexing. Elastic
reflex of latticed coordinates.
Dance of thought in language.
The evening symphony.

[10] Psyche*

In the plants' sightless kingdom
each calyx is a chrysalis
inside which blind Chance
mixes a haphazard palette, until
one day the petals burst
into flightless butterflies.
We don't see what colours our lives have.

* ψυχή n.f.   life; life-breath; soul; butterfly.

Snow

Talc creaks underfoot.
It has earthed the light,
bruising the clouds to iodine.
Bandaged cars are labouring up
a road made unfamiliar.
Somewhere, a tree sneezes.

Our scalded hands can't get enough
of compacting cotton.
Breath comes sharp as a newborn's.
This is what new love is:
the world turned upside down;
a slap to the senses.

The Goat

Along with the bell's
clattering monotony
goat carries its own
hot stink of the self-
sufficient, a thick pelt
thrown like a shag-pile
over a horse of solid
muscle.
          The slit-eye tilts
a world made steep,
capricious as its own
high rock-leaps. Lascivious,
chewing the rough cud of
bracken; tin-cans; solitude;
it bleats out its own thin
song of perseverance,
as old as Adam.

Grand Bazaar, Istanbul

Suddenly the senses are ablaze: scent
has tumbled into an Aladdin's cave
that illumines a trove of memory.
Everywhere is abundance:
baskets of chillies, red-toothed, green;
mahogany-beads of roasted Arabica;
clove-maces for miniature knights;
and glowing filaments of saffron.

Stacked canvas overspills its cargo:
cayenne; turmeric; cumin; paprika;
into pigments of the Old Masters
where the air is charged with
a hundred-tongued haggling.
Everywhere is bustle. The palate
is pollen-quickened, and all consciousness
scintillates with olfactory promise.

Lobster Trap

Contemplate the nightmare of
this dripping contraption down
on the sightless floor; how
once inside its cunning
the lobster is obsolete,
a pauldron, say, or gauntlet.

Popeyed, long-antennaed,
tentative and spanner-handed,
it awaits the scalding air,
helpless as an unhorsed knight
unable to slip the hindrance
of stiff-jointed armour.

Mellifont Abbey

The glade is loud with the zeal of bees.
No doubt disturbs their dogmatic drone.
They fumble inside auricular lilies
drunk on summer's insistent song.
The cellular mind is ignorant
how nature finds the comb unshaped
and in its wax her lattice stamps:
habit, the extent of apian faith.

Within the hive's monastic order
what impulse fires the royal alembics?
What spell refines the cloying amber
gilding the buff prismatic chambers?
What hex made eyeless petals mix
the hectic hues, to goad such ardour?

Cycles

One day more; and one day less.
Piles of leaves smoulder, and the wind
taking their blue scarves of smoke
turns a colder eye to us.

The world knows nothing as wondrous
as the warm watch hidden in your breast
that numbers each moment: this one; this one;
under the slow circle of the zodiac.

Piles of words smoulder, and old love
hangs in the air like a sentence.

Insomniac

Silence is aspirate.
It fills his room with
whispering.

The night tosses about
restless as dark foam,
and mind flits like a bat
from thought to thought.

In all this movement
only the body strives
for perfect stillness.

The body,
weary as a vessel
in which the ballast has shifted.
The head reels with the problem
of finding a lie
to accommodate its list.

The head reels, and the eyes
ache at the spin of hours,
until daylight grounds
mind, eye, body
on a shallow sand-bank.

The sun finds him
rising to his feet,
a shipwrecked man.

Anxiety

jittery spirit
                    flibbertigibbet
frittering minutes,

                  caged bird flitting
against my ribcage,
                flighty caffeine-
fired sprite,

give me a minute
                to calm my breath
to still the hammer
                of a skittish heart

a little minute
                      to come
to a decision

Wordplay

Sometimes, stark as a wood-cut, a word
stamps the world; the axe connects with its
echo's concentric backbite; no shadow,
however fleet, outruns the point of the
plunging javelin; and a poem hits its mark.

Sometimes, wanton as bees, words
stumble drunk in promiscuous pollen;
bedazzled by heraldry no plainer to decrypt
than birdsong's calligraphy. When these return,
the skull is gilded by their hubbub.

Precision contrives the prismatic comb
that libertine thoughts might honey it.

Oghma's Gift

Of all the gods had offered, he asked for this:
to understand the languages of trees.
About the boundless world, the vagrant winds
gather and distribute, but only yield
their words where trees are, gifting each to each.
Teach me, he said, the willow's soughing leaves,
the white-barked birch's whisper, the beech's
rustling, summer susurrate; winter fricative.
Teach me the knowledge of the gnarled oak
and gossip of the garrulous ivy.
That night he dreamt a herringbone of twigs
of eighteen trees, the tines of a rake, comb-teeth
to tease unruly Gaelic. Before he woke,
he scored them on the trial-piece of his forearm.

Jazz Trio

a spinal
    column   boom bass
    wrenched   cavernous
    from a   throbbing
    hunchback;   sonorous
    mouth orchid   thrumming
    dipped in   broke from
    liquid brass;   round hip
but when music   mahogany
touch the vertebrae   leaning
oh! that tenor   museum piece
    saxophone   strum
    curve   thump
    up like   strum
tobacco   thump
    smoke   yeah

    the great black bivalve prised anatomically open
    to
    bare sinew, rigid as a river fossil in a dry gully, till
    trills of minims gurgle under dunk tumble burble
    trembling over cascading over over-scaling
    and drenching the joint

Solstice

December has cut the throat of another day.
The light bleeds away, westward,
dyeing the clouds in briefest reds.
For a week, a keen wind
has honed the moon to a blade.
There's barely a sliver remaining;
a white edge that traces an arc
haunted by the memory of the old moon.
The fields are heavy as remorse.
Pools shiver at each splash of air;
cower from the senile wind;
crust around blackened grasses.
Nothing breeds here.

Nothing breeds.
And yet, amidst this baldness —
the urgent snout; the darting beak;
black leaves flicked, stabbed, rifled —
there's something clandestine abroad:
a rumour. *Solstice.* A whispered word.
The tidal moon is pregnant with it,
and cradles in her arc the print of the full.
Hedges are raising wicker fingers
to sift the zodiac's turning braille
for myths of recurrence.
Even the frost seems cold only with waiting.

It's we that grow old, not the world.
All about, nature wheels on axes of return.
Our charge is set for a single firing
before we fall to ashes.
Still we blaze up, red in the knowledge
that the maths that governs our span is strictly linear.
It carries within it the term of its own decay,
implacable as treason.

That treason is our glory.

Icarus

What he didn't know, but I knew,
was that with each ascent
of a higher contour of air
the light grows more gelid.

Old, guileful man!
I watched, far below, his flight
feathers barely sustained
above the jealous sea spray.

Now, from beyond the horizon
I allow him his bar-room story
of how I plunged headlong
into the labyrinth of waves.

Plumage and wax are concealed.
I'll not rise against his testament.

Life-Drawing

The easels are a shield-wall
about the model's nakedness.
Charcoal smuts darken paper
with cave-dweller daubs. Burnt twigs
squeak and shiver.
                    But somehow,
beneath the pubescent sootfall lies
the smudged line's insistence
that substance be hatched
out of nothing but shadow,
and the brooding imagination.

Cliff Walk, December

Marbled as quartz, the susurrant sea
rushes its incessant consonant
across feudal rocks. A gust tugs fluff
from the jostling. The sky is brindled:
sullen light contending with the dark.
I am far above the feuding guillemots,
the gannets, the cormorants' cruciform patience.
The mind moves on a higher contour.
Somewhere, though, a lobster boat
is rolling its indefatigable burble
round a cove's reverberant throat.

MOON

round
  soundless
      mouth

leprosy
has whittled the skin
from the
                lunar face
      leaving her
skull naked

night after night
  her   eyeball's
  Medusa gape is
    white as blindness
         glacial as space
            dry as eczema

methodical
      periodic
        she emerges from
            tonight's tulle
      a powdered diva
    psychotic
menopausal

          only
     the moths'
soft antennae
still attend
    her stellar
        aria

even Death has abandoned her

Death Watch

One year was

        all the doctors gave.

Days,

        he envies everyone

their hoard of time.

        Past has no substance.

Future, gangrenous,

        is to be severed.

Mornings,

        solitude rises with him

like an allegory.

        Friends shy away.

He's begun to resemble

        ambition's corpse.

And nights,

        his mind is a miser's,

tormented by rumour:

        By the ticking

of the clock…

        By the tickling

of the clock…

        By the tricking

of the clock…

        By the trickling

of the clock…

Family Album

'...man den Tod in sich hatte wie die Frucht den Kern.'

— Rainer Maria Rilke

Here, everything is exterior.
To all else the shutter is indifferent.
Here is Zeno's riddle: the moment stopped;
the still, cut from the living reel.
This is my sister; this, my mother.

What if the negative had foreseen,
with the ghost-eye of a radiograph,
that blind tumescence, Death's foetus,
already shadowing their candid flesh
like a premonition?

Power Cut

Suddenly the house was dark, deaf.
The TV popped, shrank to a dot.
Shocked by the lack we sat up,
at sea in the ink-blot black.
After a moment, the radiator
gave out a long tut-tut-tut.
Then our fingers were touching.
The world had grown transgressive
as a night slept outside.
The dormant fire began to pulse
shadows across the ceiling; in its heart
lustre blushed over the surface like
wind on water. The chimney gurgled.
And we were children again
for as long as it lasted.
More than the ash died, the instant
the room flickered back to life.

Commonplace

Nowadays, it has become a commonplace
to say the evening lies anaesthetised,
and awaits only the surgeon's knife
to kill it off;
or that the sky is a television screen,
tuned to a dead channel.

These days, there is nothing in the least surprising
about the chance encounter,
the umbrella, the sewing machine,
and it has even become a commonplace
a standard of post-modern wit
to say that everything changes,
except for the *avant-garde.*

Nowadays, what would be truly surprising
would be to stumble upon a rose
neither synthetic nor genetically enhanced,
a real-life rose, just coming into bud,
that was as seductive, pert and perfectly formed
as that pubescent-girl-in-the-poster's
provocative little pout.

Estuary

Daylight drains into the sea's radiance.
The mackerel sky can no more retain it
than we can hold the moment. Now,
light lies in shards on corrugated mudflats
where all day, a party of oyster-catchers
darted like animated sewing-machines
to tack down the tidal filigree.
Now the mudflats are empty.
Dusk has begun to silt up, and you'd think
the place could not be more desolate,
when a curlew's ululation reverberates
beyond a heron's hunched endurance
across the inconsolable sunset.

Plagiarist

He is patient as an angler.
The pen is poised, an alert dart
over a motionless page,
as though he sees shadows
moving beneath the surface.

All about the walls of the study
his books watch him.
The stillness of the scene
gives the impression
that a miracle is taking place:
that under his transfixed eye,
under his devout patience,
the stubborn paper is obtaining
the milk translucence of candle-wax,
or of a Chinese figurine.

The books know better.

They know he is old with waiting.
They know he no longer believes
in movement; in shadows.
So, out of pity perhaps,
they send old thoughts
chasing like afterimages
across the whiteness.

Such scraps sustain him.

Revolutionary

The year closes in on a winter palette,
daubs the fields in motley: ochres; umbers;
burnt sienna. Piebald greens are subdued;
gold-leaf, stripped from wind-torn trees,
tarnishes amidst rust and russet.
Only the stubborn hedgerows cling
to shivering yellows; to a bloodline of berries.
November has sloughed off its dead skin.
Over the pavements, an invasion
of *rus in urbe*: wind-snakes twist
in intricate braids, quick and brazen
as the dance of a harlequinade.

Reduced to Clear

Like something half-hatched
or premature, trailing
the open cocoon along
pavements neon-stained
and uninterested. Like litter
the street-sweepers haven't lifted.

Like an afterbirth of the city,
stubborn and unruly as graffiti
on its dreams in glass and asphalt.
Like the return of the repressed,
the ghost of the life not lived,
anaemic, persistent as guilt.

the red and the black

in the spin of the wheel
in the heart's hot embers
in the fall of trumps
in the eye of a sanctuary-lamp
in anger's shadow
in the soul of wine
in a rose's hundred eyelids
in the blood-pulse
in our wounded loves

Famine Statues

No drones over moonscape cities.
No ticker-taping newsfeed.
The celluloid unhaunted.
A silent people.

What would they tell us?
Those years the drills were blight-stalked
the land expelled them
in dry retches.

With wind bellying the canvas west
they made bare ballast in the holds
of coffin-ships, in whose wake
the throats of our harbours closed.

Fusiliers' Arch

'Treason is a matter of dates,' said Talleyrand,
though the citation is in dispute.
Who will remember, passing through this gate,
the Dublin dead who trekked across a veldt
to hunt the recusant Boer? 'Traitors,'
the Redmondites taunted, and that
vain-glorious lout, MacBride, took pot-shots
at their columns. Now, to England's distress,
a shift of Teutonic plates has brought
slaughter to the fault-lines of Empire,
who can tell traitor from patriot?
Redmond cries 'Revenge poor outraged Belgium!'
though Casement was knighted for charting
the darkness in their hearts. Now Casement's taken,
and Markievicz, entrenched in the Green,
is drawing fire; Truth, that casualty,
lies under this granite Arch.

The Dead Zoo

Mausoleum to the dying arts
of taxonomy, taxidermy,
philately, cabinet-making.
An exoskeleton, to contain
the accumulation of exhibits
in support of Mr Darwin's thesis:
the trophy heads of ruminants;
the badly upholstered apes;
the trays of assorted beetles;
the cochlea of a fossil, and
a complete set of surgical bills:
spatula and forceps and tweezers;
fashioned to probe the intimacies
of the cockle's inner ear.
What religion could remain deaf
to such meticulous cataloguing?
To cap it all, hung from a trapeze
an assemblage of whale-bone, quaint
as any contraption dreamed up by da Vinci,
as if to demonstrate, summing up,
that Nature has a Renaissance mind
and inexhaustible patience.

Text

'Is not parchment made of sheepskins?'
'Ay, my lord, and of calf-skins too.'
'They are sheep and calves which seek out assurance in that.'
(Hamlet)

Snail-shards on a song-thrush anvil;
Scaffold of a leaf, lax in puddle-silt;
Sill of wasp-husks, weightless as chaff;
Coarse fabric of roots through loam;
Moss-upholstered bones of oak
And the obduracy of fossils affirm
All things seek to persist. So phantoms,
Penned behind lines of syntax,
Endure here, hollow-eyed as Yorick.

Script

Dance of thought in language
by which thought becomes visible,
stretching the sinews of syntax,
the verb-threads, the nodal nouns
so the net approximates the motion.

The pen fixes it, casts
its shadow on the page an instant;
a contour map, a set of coordinates,
an anatomy to guess at
until the cast begins to dance.

The Injunction

Some nights, the pilot of an LED
leads back through the chambers of memory
to the votive green in the *Telefunken,*
a tabernacle to West German *Gesellschaft*
that stood sentinel over the years of
Beckenbauer and the Baader-Meinhof.

The radio was one thing. We could,
if asked, urge the needle across
Luxembourg Berlin Oslo Wien.
The turntable, upon which father
would lay a *Deutsche Grammophon,*
hawed, dusted on reverent forearm,
was, though, strictly off limits.

Still it reverberates
like a paternal caveat:
the cough of the stylus defluffed;
the circuitry clearing its throat;
the expectant static...

Restless

A sea marbled like meat.
A restless sea. You stop,
and stop me, eyes shaded.
There's someone in there...

That's not a person. It's a buoy!
The wind tugs words like gulls
out over the rolling sibilance;
our anoraks, loud in our ears.

No! Beyond the buoy.
You grip my arm. *There, see?*
And there is something, not yet someone,
tiny in the huge turmoil.

It's not, I say again, less sure.
Less sure of myself, too;
and of us,
with sea and wind and world enormous about us.

ACKNOWLEDGEMENTS

Acknowledgements are due to the following publications in which versions of some of these poems first appeared: *Poetry Ireland Review*; *The Lake*; *Oxford University Four Corners*; *The Pickled Body*; *Boyne Berries*; *The Stinging Fly*; *WOW! Anthology 2015*; *Wild Atlantic Way 2015*; *Canterbury Poet of the Year 2015 & 2016*; *Honest Ulsterman*; *The Level Crossing*; *The Luxembourg Review*; *Bare Hands*; *The Irish Times*; *Prelude Magazine* and *Into the Void*.

'The Dogfish' was shortlisted for the 2015 Words on the Waves Award and the 2016 Baileborough Award; 'Insomnia' was shortlisted for the 2016 Phizzfest Award; 'All the Dead Voices' was shortlisted for the 2015 Doolin Poetry Award; '*Ráithín an Chloig*, Bray' won the 2014 Phizzfest Award; 'Depredation' won the 2016 Ballyroan Award; 'Estuary' came 2nd in the 2015 Ballyroan Award; 'Exodus' was runner-up in the iYeats Award; 'Solstice' won the 2016 Baileborough Award and was a runner-up for the 2015 David Burland Award; and 'Father' was shortlisted for the 2016 North West Words and Donegal Creameries Aurivo Poetry Competition.

I'd like to thank all those who have been so generous in supporting my poetry down the years: my family and friends, my lovely wife Tanya, the Irish Writers' Centre, the Arts Council, Noel King of Doghouse Books, John Walsh and Lisa Frank, John F. Deane, Noel Duffy, Breda Wall Ryan and so many others.

DAVID BUTLER is a novelist, poet and playwright. The most recent of his three published novels, *City of Dis* (New Island), was shortlisted for the 2015 Kerry Group Irish Novel of the Year. Doghouse Books brought out his first poetry collection, *Via Crucis,* in 2011, while a short-story collection, *No Greater Love,* was published in London by Ward Wood in 2013. In 2016 David received a Per Cent Literary Arts Commission to compose a poetry sequence for Blackrock Library. Literary prizes include the Fish International Award for the short story, the SCDA, Cork Arts Theatre and British Theatre Challenge for drama, and the Féile Filíochta, Ted McNulty and Brendan Kennelly awards for poetry. David lives in Bray with wife and fellow author, Tanya Farrelly.